7 EASY WAYS
TO ACQUIRE
GREAT WEALTH

Copyright @ 2023 by Israel Joshua Chukwubueze

All rights reserved, no portion of this book may be reproduced, stored in a retrieval system, or transmitted in any form or by any means – electronic, mechanical, photocopy, recording, scanning, or other except for brief quotations in critical reviews or articles, without the prior written permission of the publisher.

This book may be purchased in bulk for educational, business, fundraising, or sales promotional use.

ISBN:

Published by: **Ekesy In-Outdoor Company**

10B, Mufutau Opeifa Street, Oke-Odo, Ile-Epo B/Stop, Alimosho, Lagos, Nigeria

ISREAL JOSHUA CHUKWUBUEZE

Email: ekesygroup@gmail.com

Tel: 08038154459, 08132228534

Printed by: **Demrok Prints**

For information, please contact us @

ekesygroup@gmail.com

israeljoshua.com.ng

Call: 08064342968, 08038154459

WATSAPP: 08132228534

TABLE OF CONTENTS

DEDICATION

ACKNOWLEDGEMENT

FOREWORD

PREFACE

INTRODUCTION

CHAPTER ONE: THE LAW OF 10%; SAVE 10% OF ALL INCOME

CHAPTER TWO: SETTING A BUDGET: THE KEY TO CONSISTENTLY SAVING 10%

CHAPTER THREE: INVESTMENT 101: PUTTING YOUR MONEY TO WORK

CHAPTER FOUR: MANAGING RISK: PROTECTING YOUR INVESTMENT

CHAPTER FIVE: THE POWER OF HOME OWNERSHIP: BUILDING WEALTH THROUGH REAL ESTATE

CHAPTER SIX: RETIREMENT PLANNING AND INSURANCE: PROTECTING YOUR FUTURE

CHAPTER SEVEN: LIFELONG LEARNING: INCREASING YOUR EARNING POTENTIAL

7 More Steps/Chapters Bonuses

CHAPTER EIGHT: MAXIMIZING YOUR INCOME: NEGOTIATING SALARIES AND RAISES

CHAPTER NINE: DEBT MANAGEMENT: GETTING OUT OF DEBT AND STAYING OUT

CHAPTER TEN: TAX PLANNING: MAXIMIZING YOUR DEDUCTIONS AND CREDITS

CHAPTER ELEVEN: REAL ESTATE INVESTING: BUILDING WEALTH THROUGH PROPERTY

CHAPTER TWELVE: STOCK MARKET INVESTING: BUILDING WEALTH THROUGH EQUITIES

CHAPTER THIRTEEN: ENTREPRENEURSHIP: BUILDING WEALTH THROUGH STARTING A BUSINESS

CHAPTER FOURTEEN: CONCLUSION: PUTTING IT ALL TOGETHER

DEDICATION

This book is dedicated to my God, Mom, Kids, Friends, Colleagues and my humble Staff.

And everyone who wish me well.

ACKNOWLEDGEMENT

I owe special thanks to several people who made it possible for me to complete this book in the face of challenges and several tight responsibilities.

And thanks to my mom, who have always helped me in taking care of my kids; the love is beyond words.

And to my kids, who understand about the many nights and weekends that I have spent working on this book; I appreciate your patience.

And to God, may all glory be to Him.

FOREWORD

Wealth has to remain arguably one of the essential ingredients in living; without money, one cannot attain a certain societal height or even survive. Wealth is everything that everyone needs to live life, comfortably or sustainably. We can argue other things, but money controls virtually everything.

This book envisaged the ways one can acquire wealth legitimately and smartly. With the introduction of technology, young men and women are taking the opportunity to learn things that will advance their knowledge also, expose them to new opportunities and that's what this book has been able to achieve by ensuring the right tools are being used in the right ways to acquire wealth. This isn't another book that's entered to motivate people, no, this isn't another acquire to perspire to aspire – this is in real-time, the real deal to make money legitimately and smartly.

The author is a good friend of mine and we've known each other for a period of more than five years, and I can affirm and attest that his great wealth of experience in financial literacy and liberation is indubitably rich. He has outlined information with experiences and also, practically, put that information in a way it will be made easy for anyone seeking financial freedom.

Reading this book, **7 Easy Ways To Acquire Great Wealth**, I know for sure, there are going to be lots of testimonies.

Happy reading!

~**Chidibere A. Okoroji,** *M.Ed*

PREFACE

This book is written to impact knowledge on financial freedom and liberation, especially during this period of economic challenges. I have been able to outline perfect solutions that will enable readers to have practical ideas on wealth creation using the 4 pillars of wealth creation as a guide.

I'm the MD/CEO of Ekesy In-Outdoor Company with brand services like eWeb9ja.com, 24000hosting.com, MamaEkene.com, and israeljoshua.com.ng.

You can browse online to confirm my claims for authentication. My official name is Christopher Ekene Okade (now Israel Joshua Chukwubueze).

This book is a collection of what I do, that changes the story of my life. Life can be more complex and you need to have a road map to get to your destination faster and easier.

Success and happiness require great and smart work; failure and struggling require no effort but, which one of them will you choose? I choose great and smart work because I know for sure that the rewards are great.

I will recommend this book to those who want to create wealth and be successful and comfortable.

The book is loaded with information on life experiences,

exposure, knowledge, and other study references from successful men and women. This book will improve and change your mind on our wealth and wealth creation.

~Israel Joshua Chukwubueze

INTRODUCTION

If you learn and practices what you will read in this book, you will definitely find happiness & joy and you will become successful and wealthy.

The steps are easy but hard to start but if you can start, then later you will form the habit and when it becomes your habit then that is when your joy, happiness and peace will set in.

My Name is Isreal Joshua Chukwubueze and I'm formerly known as Christopher Ekene Okade. Once upon a time I was struggling in life financially and I have always wanted to become successful person.

I was not born with a silver spoon and I don't have any money, I have worked for over 15yrs+ in different places of work and I have nothing to show for it, then I decided to start my own business so that I can become rich.

Yes, I started my business with just $3 and a borrowed laptop and I break through; and after which I think I'm successful I was still struggling financially. Though my level had improved and I also have staffs that are working for me, but yet I was still struggling financially and am not happy about it.

Yes, I'm successful but I want more, I want to be wealthy, to accumulate more money. Then one day, I stormed into a Big Secret that I want to share with you in this Book what I found out. Maybe you too are in this position, what you will learn in this book will improve everything.

Though these secrets are not secrets at all, you may know it but you have never thought deeply about it. And it is easy but it may be hard to start, but once you start it, you will first find happiness, knowing that one day you will achieve that which your heart desired

CHAPTER ONE:

THE LAW OF 10%: SAVE 10% OF ALL YOUR INCOME

Saving money is the first step towards building wealth. The Law of 10% states that you should save 10% of all your income, no matter how small or large it is. This may seem like a small amount, but over time, it can add up to a significant sum of money. In this chapter, we will discuss the importance of saving 10% of your income and provide strategies for making it a habit.

The Importance of Saving 10% of Your Income

1. Building an emergency fund: An emergency fund is a savings account set aside for unexpected expenses, such as a medical emergency or job loss. By saving 10% of your income, you can build an emergency fund that can provide financial security in case of unexpected events.

2. Investing for the future: Saving 10% of your income allows you to invest in your future by setting money aside for retirement, a child's education, or other long-term goals.

3. Creating financial freedom: By saving 10% of your income, you can create financial freedom, which means having enough money to cover your expenses without needing to rely on a steady income.

Strategies for Making Saving 10% of Your Income a Habit

1. Automate your savings: Set up automatic transfers from

your checking account to your savings account each month. This way, you won't have to remember to transfer money manually and you'll be less likely to spend it.

2. Start small: If 10% seems like too much to save initially, start with a smaller percentage and increase it as you get comfortable.

3. Make a budget: Create a budget that includes a savings category. By setting aside money for savings in your budget, you'll be less likely to spend it on other things.

4. Find ways to increase your income: Look for ways to increase your income, such as asking for a raise or taking on a side hustle.

5. Track your progress: Keep track of your savings progress and set goals for yourself. This will help you stay motivated and on track.

Saving 10% of your income may seem like a small amount, but over time, it can add up to a significant sum of money. By making saving a habit, you can build an emergency fund, invest in your future, and create financial freedom. Remember, the key to saving money is consistency. Start small, automate your savings, make a budget, and track your progress.

First step to build my wealth. Save every 10% of your income. Every man has one source or the other to make or get money. As a student, one of your sources of getting money can be from your pocket money or other money from your families or relatives. As a salary earner, your first source of income is from your salary. As a handy worker, your source of income is from your handwork and services. As a trader, your source of income is from the profit of your sales As a Business man, your sources of income are from your business transactions.

Therefore, every man and woman on this planet earth has one way or the other of getting money into the hands and pockets.

Then if that is the case, why are some people wealthier than the other?

The answer is simple!

The wealthy people have that knowledge or secret of keeping money and growing money.

The first law of wealth: save money 10% of income.

Example 1: If you save $1000 every month, how much will you have in 5 years? $1,000 X 12 months = $12,000.
$12,000 X 5 = $60,000

Example 2: If you save $2,000 every month, how much will you have in 10 years? $2000 X 12 months = $24,000.
$24,000 X 10 years = $240,000

Example 3: If you save $10,000 every month, how much will you have in 20 years $10,000 X 12 months = $120,000.
$120,000 X 20years = $2,400,000.

Really, so you can see that you can save up to become a millionaire.

Every great wealth started by these simple steps. The law of 10%, simply means "Pay yourself 1st".

Now most people will complain that the money they are making or earning is not enough for them to spend, but the simple truth is that money will never be enough for every man and woman to spend.

So if this is the case, what should we do?
The answer is simple, every time you get money into your account, just divide the money into ten places and take one tenth of the money and put it away into your savings account.

Then you can spend the rest the way you want it.

Talking about savings account, for this great purpose of growing wealth, I advice that you use a separate account for this purpose, if you have many account, dedicate one of your account for your financing freedom.

And if you have only one account, I recommend that you should get a new account for this purpose.

You can if you want to call this account: **Freedom Account.** Success is a habit and failure is also a habit. If you can form the habit of saving every 10% of your income, you definitely develop the habit of successful and wealthy people.

Therefore no matter who you are, whether a student, salary earner, handy worker, businessmen & women, get a separate account for your financial freedom and save every 10% of your income.

This is the beginning of wealth, joy, happiness and success! Men that have their money saved in their account are men of boosted energy and ego. And men without money are weak and broke in the spirit.

Wealth is not how much you make but how much you keep.

To be happy and wealthy, pay yourself first by keeping 10% of your income to yourself.

My recommendation of saving and expenses:

Divide your income into 10, then save:
- 10% = financial freedom
- 10% = special projects and spending
- 10% = tithe, offering, donation and charity purpose.
- Then spend the remaining 70% for all your normal and day to day spending.
- Special Projects / Funding: Your special projects or

spending can be anything spending that you may not be able to pull out funds immediately to execute; therefore you can save towards these projects so that it does not affect your day-to-day spending

For example maybe you want to bur a laptop, generator, home and office appliances, special education and carrier funding, etc, you can save up this 10% to execute this project/funding.

I also recommend to you to open a separate account for this purpose Then the last 10% for tithes, offering, donation and charity purpose of giving to churches and the needy.

It is profitable, that we also help the less privilege around us, this third 10% can be save up for these purposes.

In summary, the first step to building wealth is to save 10% of all your income. This is known as the "law of 10%."

By consistently saving 10% of your income, you will be able to accumulate wealth over time. It's important to have a separate savings account for this purpose, and to make sure you pay yourself first before spending the rest of your money.

Additionally, dividing your income into three parts, where 10% is saved for financial freedom, 10% for special projects and spending, and 10% for tithes, offerings, donations, and charity is a good way to keep your finances organized.

It is also important to remember that wealth is not about how much you make, but how much you keep, and that developing the habit of saving is key to achieving financial success.

ISREAL JOSHUA CHUKWUBUEZE

CHAPTER TWO:

"Setting a Budget: The Key to Consistently Saving 10%"

Budgeting is an essential part of achieving financial success and building wealth. It's the key to consistently saving 10% of your income, which is the first step towards accumulating wealth.

In this chapter, we will discuss the importance of setting a budget, the benefits it can bring, and the strategies you can use to create and stick to a budget.

Why is setting a budget important?
A budget is a plan for how you will spend your money. It's like a map that guides you towards your financial goals. Without a budget, it's easy to overspend and find yourself in debt.

By setting a budget, you'll be able to see where your money is going, identify areas where you can cut back, and make sure you're saving enough to reach your financial goals.

Benefits of budgeting
- It helps you save money: One of the most obvious benefits of budgeting is that it helps you save money. By setting a budget, you'll be able to see where your money is going and make sure you're putting enough into savings.
- It helps you pay off debt: Another benefit of budgeting is that it can help you pay off debt. By identifying areas where you're overspending, you can redirect that money towards paying off

your debts.
- It helps you reach your financial goals: Setting a budget also helps you reach your financial goals. By allocating money towards specific goals, you'll be able to see how much you need to save and by when.
- It helps you feel more in control of your money: Budgeting also helps you feel more in control of your money. When you know where your money is going, you're less likely to feel overwhelmed by bills and expenses.

Strategies for creating and sticking to a budget

1. Start by setting financial goals: Before you create a budget, it's important to set some financial goals. What do you want to achieve financially? Do you want to save for a down payment on a house, pay off your credit card debt, or save for retirement? By setting specific financial goals, you'll be able to create a budget that will help you achieve them.

2. Track your expenses: The next step is to track your expenses. This will help you see where your money is going and identify areas where you can cut back. You can use a budgeting app or spreadsheet, or simply write down your expenses in a notebook.

3. Set a spending limit for each category: Once you've tracked your expenses, set a spending limit for each category. For example, you might set a limit of $50 per month for entertainment, $150 for groceries, and $200 for rent.

4. Automate your savings: Another strategy for sticking to a budget is to automate your savings. By setting up automatic transfers to your savings account, you'll be less likely to forget to save.

5. Revisit and adjust your budget regularly: It's important to revisit your budget regularly and adjust it as necessary. Your

expenses will change over time, so it's important to make sure your budget reflects that.

6. Prioritize your spending: Finally, prioritize your spending. Make sure you're spending money on the things that are most important to you. For example, if saving for a down payment on a house is a priority, make sure you're putting enough money towards that goal.

In conclusion, setting a budget is crucial to achieving financial success and building wealth. By consistently saving 10% of your income, you'll be able to accumulate wealth over time.

CHAPTER THREE:

"Investment 101: Putting Your Money to Work"

Investing is an essential part of building wealth and achieving financial success. It's the next step after saving 10% of your income, and it allows your money to grow and compound over time.

In this chapter, we will discuss the basics of investing, the different types of investments available, and the strategies you can use to make your money work for you.

Why is investing important?

Investing is important because it allows your money to grow over time. If you simply save your money in a savings account, it will earn a small amount of interest, but the value of your money will not grow much over time. By investing your money in a variety of different assets, you can earn a higher return and increase the value of your money over time.

Different types of investments

1. Stocks: Stocks, also known as equities, represent ownership in a company. When you buy a stock, you become a shareholder in that company, and you're entitled to a share of the company's profits. Stocks can be a good investment because they have the potential to earn a higher return than

savings accounts, but they also come with more risk.

2. Bonds: Bonds are debt securities issued by governments or companies. When you buy a bond, you're lending money to the issuer, and they promise to pay you back with interest. Bonds are generally considered to be less risky than stocks, but they also tend to earn a lower return.

3. Real estate: Real estate investing involves buying property with the goal of earning rental income or reselling the property for a profit. Real estate can be a great investment, but it also comes with more risk and requires more capital upfront.

4. Mutual funds: Mutual funds are a type of investment that pools money from a large number of investors and invests it in a variety of stocks, bonds, and other securities. Mutual funds are managed by professional fund managers, and they can be a good option for investors who want to diversify their portfolio without having to pick individual stocks or bonds.

5. Cryptocurrency: Cryptocurrency is a digital currency that uses cryptography for security. Cryptocurrency is decentralized and not controlled by any government or institution. Bitcoin, Ethereum, and Litecoin are popular examples of cryptocurrency, they're considered as a high-risk investment but with potential high returns.

Strategies for investing
1. Diversify your portfolio: One of the most important strategies for investing is to diversify your portfolio. By investing in a variety of different assets, you can spread your risk and increase your chances of earning a good return.

2. Invest for the long-term: Investing is not a get-rich-quick

scheme, it is a long-term strategy. Investing in high-growth assets like stocks or real estate may be volatile in the short-term, but over the long-term, they have the potential to earn high returns. By investing for the long-term, you'll be able to ride out market fluctuations and earn a higher return on your investment.

3. Start small and gradually increase your investment: If you're new to investing, it's best to start small and gradually increase your investment as you gain more experience and confidence. You can start by investing a small amount of money in a mutual fund or exchange-traded fund (ETF), and then gradually increase your investment as you learn more about different investment options.

4. Learn about the different investment options: It's important to educate yourself about the different types of investments available. You should learn about the risks and rewards of each investment option, and how they fit into your overall investment strategy.

5. Understand the risks and rewards of each investment: Every investment comes with its own set of risks and rewards. It's important to understand the risks involved with each investment and how they fit into your overall investment strategy. For example, stocks may offer a higher return but also come with more risk than bonds.

In conclusion, investing is an essential part of building wealth and achieving financial success. It allows your money to grow and compound over time, and it is the next step after saving 10% of your income. There are a variety of different types of investments available, each with their own set of risks and rewards. To make the most of your investment, it's important to diversify your portfolio, invest for the long-term, start small and gradually increase your investment, educate yourself about the different investment options, and understand the risks and rewards of each investment.

By following these strategies, you'll be able to make your money work for you and achieve your financial goals.

CHAPTER FOUR:

"Managing Risk: Protecting Your Investment"

Investing always comes with some level of risk. It's important to understand the different types of risks involved in order to make informed decisions and protect your investment. In this chapter, we will discuss the different types of risks associated with investing and strategies for managing them.

Types of Investment Risks

1. Market risk: Market risk is the risk that the value of your investment will decrease due to changes in the overall market. This risk is present in all investments, and it's impossible to eliminate it completely. However, diversifying your portfolio and investing in a variety of different assets can help to spread the risk.

2. Credit risk: Credit risk is the risk that the issuer of an investment will default on their debt obligations. This risk is present in investments such as bonds, where you're lending money to the issuer. To manage credit risk, it's important to invest in bonds issued by companies or governments with a strong credit rating.

3. Interest rate risk: Interest rate risk is the risk that the value of your investment will decrease due to changes in interest rates. This risk is present in investments such as bonds, where the value of the bond decreases as interest rates

rise. To manage interest rate risk, you can invest in bonds with shorter maturities or bond funds that hold a variety of bonds with different maturities.

4. Liquidity risk: Liquidity risk is the risk that you won't be able to sell your investment quickly or at a fair price. This risk is present in investments such as real estate or collectibles, which can be difficult to sell quickly. To manage liquidity risk, you should only invest in assets that are easily and quickly convertable to cash.

5. Currency risk: Currency risk is the risk that changes in currency exchange rates will affect the value of your investment. This risk is present when you invest in assets denominated in a foreign currency. To manage currency risk, you can invest in assets denominated in your home currency or use currency hedging strategies.

Strategies for Managing Risk

1. Diversify your portfolio: Diversifying your portfolio is one of the most effective ways to manage risk. By investing in a variety of different assets, you can spread your risk and increase your chances of earning a good return.

2. Invest in assets with low correlation: Investing in assets that have a low correlation to each other can also help to manage risk. For example, stocks and bonds have a low correlation, so investing in both can help to spread your risk.

3. Use stop-loss orders: Stop-loss orders are a strategy that can help to manage risk by automatically selling an investment when it reaches a certain price. This can help to limit losses if the value of the investment decreases.

4. Use hedging strategies: Hedging strategies such as

options or futures contracts can help to manage risk by providing a way to offset potential losses in one investment with gains in another.

5. Regularly review and rebalance your portfolio: Regularly reviewing and rebalancing your portfolio can help to manage risk by ensuring that your investments are aligned with your risk tolerance and investment goals.

6. Be mindful of your emotions: Be aware of your emotions when making investment decisions. Avoid making impulsive decisions based on fear or greed, instead, stick to a well-thought-out investment strategy.

7. Seek professional advice: Consider seeking professional financial advice when making investment decisions. A financial advisor can help you understand the risks associated with different investments and develop a risk management strategy that is tailored to your needs and goals.

It's important to remember that there's no such thing as a risk-free investment. However, by understanding the different types of risks and implementing strategies to manage them, you can protect your investment and increase your chances of achieving your financial goals.

CHAPTER FIVE:

"The Power of Home Ownership: Building Wealth through Real Estate"

Homeownership is a powerful tool for building wealth. Not only does owning a home provide a stable living environment and a sense of pride and accomplishment, but it can also be a valuable investment that can appreciate in value over time. In this chapter, we will explore the benefits of home ownership and the strategies for building wealth through real estate.

Benefits of Homeownership

1. Appreciation: Real estate has the potential to appreciate in value over time. As the economy and housing market grows, the value of your home can increase, providing a return on your investment.

2. Tax Benefits: Owning a home comes with significant tax benefits. Mortgage interest is tax-deductible, and property taxes are also typically deductible. Additionally, if you sell your home for a profit, you may be eligible for a tax exclusion on the capital gains.

3. Forced Savings: Making a mortgage payment forces you to save money. Each mortgage payment you make goes towards paying down your mortgage, building equity in your home, and increasing your net worth.

4. Stable Living Environment: Homeownership provides

a stable living environment. Unlike renting, you have the freedom to make changes to your home and personalize it to your liking.

Strategies for Building Wealth through Real Estate

1. Invest in rental properties: Investing in rental properties can provide a steady stream of income and the potential for appreciation. Consider purchasing properties in areas with strong rental demand and a growing population.

2. Invest in fixer-upper properties: Purchasing a fixer-upper property and renovating it can be a great way to add value and increase the potential appreciation of the property.

3. Consider house flipping: House flipping involves purchasing a property, making improvements and then selling it for a profit. This can be a great way to earn a quick return on your investment, but it is important to do your research and understand the local real estate market before diving in.

4. Live in one property and rent out the others: If you own multiple properties, consider living in one and renting out the others. This can provide a steady stream of rental income, and the potential for appreciation in the value of the property you live in.

5. Don't over-leverage yourself: It's important to be mindful of the amount of debt you take on when purchasing a property. Make sure you have enough cash reserves to cover unexpected expenses and that you can comfortably make your mortgage payments.

Homeownership is a powerful tool for building wealth, but it's important to understand the risks and strategies involved. By considering the benefits and strategies discussed in this chapter, you'll be able to make informed decisions about your real estate investments and build wealth over time.

CHAPTER SIX:

"Retirement Planning and Insurance: Protecting Your Future"

Retirement planning and insurance are important components of building wealth and securing your financial future. In this chapter, we will discuss the importance of saving for retirement and the various types of insurance that can protect you and your loved ones from financial hardship.

Retirement Planning

1. Start saving early: The earlier you start saving for retirement, the more time your money has to grow. Additionally, starting to save early means you can save less each month and still reach your retirement goals.

2. Take advantage of employer-sponsored retirement plans: Many employers offer retirement plans such as 401(k)s or pension plans. These plans typically offer tax advantages and employer matching contributions, making them a valuable way to save for retirement.

3. Consider a Roth IRA: A Roth IRA is a retirement savings account that allows your money to grow tax-free and be withdrawn tax-free in retirement. This can be a valuable way to save for retirement, especially if you expect to be in a higher tax bracket in retirement.

4.   Educate yourself: Take the time to educate yourself about the different types of retirement savings accounts and investment options available. This will help you make informed decisions about where to invest your money and how to reach your retirement goals.

Insurance

Insurance is a crucial aspect of protecting your financial future. It can provide financial protection for you and your loved ones in case of unexpected events.

In this chapter, we will discuss the different types of insurance that can help protect you and your assets.

1.   Life insurance: Life insurance can provide financial protection for your loved ones in the event of your death. It can help pay for expenses such as funeral costs, outstanding debts, and living expenses for your loved ones. There are two main types of life insurance: term life insurance and whole life insurance. Term life insurance provides coverage for a specific period of time, while whole life insurance provides coverage for the entire life of the policyholder.

2.   Health insurance: Health insurance can provide financial protection for you and your family in case of unexpected medical expenses. It is important to have adequate health insurance, particularly as medical costs can be extremely high. There are two main types of health insurance: employer-sponsored plans and individual plans. Employer-sponsored plans are typically offered through an employer, while individual plans can be purchased directly from an insurance company.

3.   Disability insurance: Disability insurance can provide financial protection in case you become unable to work due to

an accident or illness. This type of insurance can help pay for living expenses and medical costs if you are unable to work.

4. Long-term care insurance: Long-term care insurance can provide financial protection in case you need assistance with daily living activities due to a chronic illness or disability. This type of insurance can help pay for expenses such as in-home care or nursing home costs.

5. Homeowners and auto insurance: Homeowners and auto insurance can provide financial protection in case of damage or loss to your property or vehicle. This type of insurance can help cover the cost of repairs or replacement.

It's important to remember that the types of insurance you need will depend on your individual circumstances and risk tolerance.

Consider your assets, income, and potential liabilities when choosing the insurance coverage that's right for you.

A financial advisor can help you determine the right insurance coverage for your specific needs and budget.

CHAPTER SEVEN:

"Lifelong Learning: Increasing Your Earning Potential"

Lifelong learning is the process of continuously acquiring new knowledge, skills, and abilities throughout one's life. In today's fast-paced and constantly changing world, it's more important than ever to continuously learn and adapt in order to be successful. In this chapter, we will discuss the importance of lifelong learning and strategies for increasing your earning potential.

The Importance of Lifelong Learning

1. Keeping up with technological advancements: Rapid advancements in technology are changing the way we work and live. To stay competitive in the job market, it's important to continuously learn about new technologies and how to use them in your field.

2. Adapting to new industries: Industries are constantly changing and evolving, and new industries are emerging all the time. To stay competitive, it's important to learn about new industries and how to adapt your skills to them.

3. Staying relevant: The job market is highly competitive, and employers are looking for individuals with the most current skills and knowledge. By continuously learning, you can stay relevant and increase your earning potential.

Strategies for Increasing Your Earning Potential

1. Formal education: Formal education, such as a college or graduate degree, can open up new career opportunities and increase your earning potential. Consider going back to school to earn a new degree or certification.

2. Professional development courses: Professional development courses can help you acquire new skills and knowledge in your field. Consider taking courses online or at a local college or university.

3. Networking: Networking with other professionals in your field can help you learn about new job opportunities, as well as new skills and knowledge. Attend conferences, join professional organizations, and attend industry events.

4. On-the-job learning: On-the-job learning can be one of the most effective ways to increase your earning potential. Seek out new responsibilities and projects at work, and take advantage of any training opportunities offered by your employer.

5. Self-directed learning: Reading books, listening to podcasts, and watching webinars on topics related to your field can be a great way to learn new information and stay up-to-date with industry trends.

In conclusion, lifelong learning is crucial for success in today's fast-paced and constantly changing world. By continuously acquiring new knowledge, skills, and abilities, you can stay relevant and competitive in the job market, and increase your earning potential over time.

In this chapter, we discussed the importance of lifelong learning and strategies for increasing your earning potential.

Formal education, professional development courses, networking, on-the-job learning, and self-directed learning are all effective ways to learn new information and stay up-to-date with industry trends.

It's important to remember that lifelong learning is a continuous process and it's never too late to start. Whether you're a student, a working professional, or a retiree, there are always opportunities to learn and grow.

Take the time to evaluate your current skills and knowledge, and identify areas where you can improve.

Then, make a plan to acquire the necessary skills and knowledge to reach your goals.

In addition, it's important to have the right mindset when it comes to learning. Be open to new ideas and experiences, and don't be afraid to step out of your comfort zone.

Embrace challenges and take risks, because it's through these experiences that you'll grow the most.

7 MORE BONUSES CHAPTERS

CHAPTER EIGHT:

"Maximizing Your Income: Negotiating Salaries And Raises"

In today's job market, it's important to know how to negotiate your salary and ask for raises in order to increase your income and build wealth. In this chapter, we'll discuss strategies for negotiating your salary and raises, as well as tips for making your case to your employer.

1. Do your research: Before negotiating your salary or asking for a raise, research the average salary for your position and industry. This will give you a baseline to work from and help you make a convincing argument for a higher salary.

2. Highlight your achievements: When asking for a raise, be sure to highlight your achievements and contributions to the company. Provide specific examples of how you have added value to the company and how your work has benefited the organization.

3. Be prepared to negotiate: When negotiating your salary, be prepared to compromise and negotiate. Be willing to consider other forms of compensation, such as additional vacation days, flexible work arrangements, or a signing bonus.

4. Be confident: When negotiating your salary or asking for a raise, be confident in your abilities and the value you bring to the company. Speak clearly and assertively, and be prepared to defend your position.

5. Timing is key: Timing is important when asking for a raise. Try to schedule your meeting when your employer is most likely to be receptive, such as after a successful project or when the company is performing well financially.

6. Look for other opportunities: If your employer is unable to offer you a raise, consider looking for other opportunities within the company or seeking out new job opportunities. Sometimes, it's better to move on to a new employer that can offer you a higher salary.

7. Be persistent: If your employer is unable to offer you a raise at this time, don't give up. Keep the conversation open and continue to demonstrate your value to the company. Eventually, your hard work and dedication will be recognized and you'll be in a better position to negotiate a higher salary.

Negotiating your salary and asking for raises can be intimidating, but it's a crucial step in maximizing your income and building wealth.

ISREAL JOSHUA CHUKWUBUEZE

CHAPTER NINE:

"DEBT MANAGEMENT: GETTING OUT OF DEBT AND STAYING OUT"

One of the biggest obstacles to building wealth is the burden of high levels of debt. In this chapter, we'll discuss strategies for getting out of debt and staying out, so you can take control of your finances and start building wealth.

1. Create a budget: The first step in getting out of debt is to create a budget. This will help you understand where your money is going and where you can cut expenses.

2. Prioritize your debts: Once you have a budget in place, prioritize your debts by interest rate. Focus on paying off the debts with the highest interest rates first, as these will be the most costly in the long run.

3. Consolidate your debts: If you have multiple debts, consider consolidating them into one loan with a lower interest rate. This can make it easier to manage your payments and potentially save you money in interest charges.

4. Consider a debt management plan: If you're struggling to make your minimum payments, consider a debt

management plan. This is a repayment plan where a credit counseling agency negotiates with your creditors to reduce your interest rates and monthly payments.

5. Stop using credit: To stay out of debt, it's important to stop using credit. This means not taking on new debt and only using cash or debit for purchases.

6. Build an emergency fund: One of the best ways to stay out of debt is to have an emergency fund in place. This will help you avoid turning to credit when unexpected expenses arise.

7. Seek professional help: If you're struggling with debt and can't seem to make progress on your own, consider seeking professional help from a financial advisor or credit counselor. They can help you create a plan to get out of debt and offer guidance and support along the way.

Managing debt is an ongoing process and it takes time, discipline and patience. But with the right strategies in place, you can take control of your finances and start building wealth. By creating a budget, prioritizing your debts, consolidating loans, seeking professional help and building an emergency fund, you can get out of debt and stay out of it for good.

CHAPTER TEN:

"Tax Planning: Maximizing Your Deductions And Credits"

Tax planning is an important aspect of building wealth, as it can help you keep more of your hard-earned money. In this chapter, we'll discuss strategies for maximizing your deductions and credits, as well as provide an overview of the tax code and common deductions and credits.

1. Understand the tax code: The first step in tax planning is to understand the tax code. This includes knowing the different tax brackets, deductions, and credits that are available to you.

2. Keep good records: To maximize your deductions and credits, it's important to keep good records. This means keeping receipts, invoices, and other documentation for all of your expenses.

3. Take advantage of deductions: There are many deductions available to taxpayers, including deductions for mortgage interest, charitable donations, and state and local taxes. Be sure to take advantage of all the deductions for which you qualify.

4. Claim credits: Credits can be even more valuable

than deductions, as they directly reduce the amount of taxes you owe. Some common credits include the Earned Income Tax Credit, Child Tax Credit, and Education Credit.

5. Plan for retirement: Tax planning for retirement is an important aspect of building wealth. Contributions to a traditional IRA or 401(k) are tax-deductible, which can help you lower your taxable income.

6. Use tax-advantaged accounts: Tax-advantaged accounts such as Health Savings Accounts (HSAs) and Flexible Spending Accounts (FSAs) can help you save money on taxes by allowing you to set aside money for medical expenses and other qualified expenses, pre-tax.

6. Keep an eye on tax law changes: Tax laws are constantly changing, and it's important to stay informed of any changes that may affect your deductions and credits. Keep an eye out for any new laws or changes to existing laws and adjust your tax planning strategies accordingly.

7. Hire a professional: Tax planning can be complex and time-consuming, especially if you have a lot of deductions and credits to claim. Consider hiring a professional tax preparer or accountant to help you navigate the tax code and maximize your deductions and credits.

8. Review your withholding: Review your withholding and make sure you're not having too much or too

little withheld from your paycheck. Having too much withheld can mean you're giving the government an interest-free loan, while having too little withheld can lead to a larger tax bill or penalties.

9. Plan ahead: Tax planning is not something you do just once a year. It's an ongoing process that should be reviewed and adjusted regularly. The earlier you start planning, the more time you have to adjust your strategies and make changes that can help you save money on taxes in the long run.

In conclusion, tax planning is an essential part of building wealth. By understanding the tax code, taking advantage of deductions and credits, and planning ahead.

CHAPTER ELEVEN:

"Real Estate Investing: Building Wealth Through Property"

Real estate investing is a popular and effective way to build wealth. In this chapter, we'll discuss strategies for building wealth through property, including how to find and evaluate properties, how to finance and manage real estate investments, and how to create a plan for long-term success.

1. Understand the market: Before investing in real estate, it's important to understand the market you're investing in. Research the area, including property values, rental rates, and trends, to determine if it's a good place to invest.

2. Find the right property: Finding the right property is key to successful real estate investing. Look for properties that are in good condition, have potential for appreciation, and are in a desirable location.

3. Evaluate the property: Once you've found a property, it's important to evaluate it thoroughly. Consider the condition of the property, the cost of repairs and renovations, and the potential income and expenses.

4. Finance your investment: There are many ways to

finance a real estate investment, including traditional mortgages, private loans, and crowdfunding. Choose the option that best fits your investment goals and risk tolerance.

5. Manage the property: Once you've purchased a property, it's important to manage it effectively. This includes finding and retaining tenants, collecting rent, and maintaining the property. Consider hiring a property management company if you don't have the time or expertise to do it yourself.

6. Create a long-term plan: Real estate investing is a long-term game. Create a plan for how you will hold and manage the property over time, including how long you plan to hold onto the property and when you plan to sell.

7. Diversify your portfolio: Diversifying your portfolio is important in any type of investing, and real estate is no exception. Spread your investments across different types of properties, locations, and markets to minimize risk.

8. Continuously educate yourself: The real estate market and laws are constantly changing. Stay informed of any changes that may affect your investments, and continuously educate yourself on new strategies and tactics for building wealth through real estate.

9. Network with other real estate investors: Building a network of other real estate investors can be incredibly valuable. They can provide valuable insights, advice

and even connect you to deals and opportunities that you may not have otherwise come across.

10. Be patient: Investing in real estate takes time and patience. Don't get discouraged if you don't see immediate returns. Building wealth through property is a long-term process and requires patience and persistence.

In conclusion, real estate investing is a powerful tool for building wealth. By understanding the market, finding the right property, evaluating it thoroughly, financing it, managing it effectively, creating a long-term plan, and continuously educating yourself, you can create a solid foundation for building wealth through property. Remember to network with other investors and be patient in your approach. With the right strategies and mindset, you can achieve financial freedom and secure your financial future through real estate investing.

ISREAL JOSHUA CHUKWUBUEZE

CHAPTER TWELVE:

"Stock Market Investing: Building Wealth Through Equities"

The stock market is a powerful tool for building wealth, but it can also be risky if you don't know what you're doing. In this chapter, we'll discuss strategies for building wealth through equities, including how to find and evaluate stocks, how to create a diversified portfolio, and how to manage risk.

1. Understand the market: Before investing in the stock market, it's important to understand how it works. Learn about the different types of stocks, how they're traded, and how to read financial statements.

2. Develop a strategy: Determine your investment goals and risk tolerance, and develop a strategy for achieving them. This may include a mix of long-term investments, short-term trades, or a combination of both.

3. Find and evaluate stocks: Research potential stocks and evaluate them based on factors such as financial performance, management, industry trends, and risk. Consider using a stock screener to narrow down your options.

4. Create a diversified portfolio: Diversifying your portfolio is key to managing risk and maximizing returns. Invest in a mix of stocks from different sectors, industries, and regions to minimize the impact of any one stock's poor performance.

5. Stay informed: Keep up with the latest financial news and market trends to stay informed about any events that may affect your investments.

6. Manage risk: No investment is without risk, and the stock market is no exception. Use risk management strategies such as stop-loss orders, hedging, and diversification to minimize the potential impact of a bad investment.

7. Have patience: Investing in the stock market takes time and patience. Don't get discouraged if you don't see immediate returns, and resist the urge to make impulsive trades based on short-term market fluctuations.

8. Continuously educate yourself: The stock market is constantly changing and evolving, so it's important to continuously educate yourself and stay informed on new strategies and tactics.

9. Consider hiring a financial advisor: If you're new to the stock market or you feel overwhelmed by the complexity of it, consider hiring a financial advisor who can help you navigate the market and develop an investment strategy that aligns with your goals.

10. Remember that past performance does not guarantee future results: Keep in mind that past performance of a stock or market is not indicative of future performance. It's important to stay vigilant and continuously evaluate your investments to ensure they align with your goals and risk tolerance.

In conclusion, investing in the stock market can be a powerful tool for building wealth, but it also comes with risks. By understanding the market, developing a strategy, finding and evaluating stocks, creating a diversified portfolio, staying informed, managing risk, being patient, and continuously educating yourself, you can increase your chances of success. Additionally, consider hiring a financial advisor and remember to keep in mind that past performance does not guarantee future results. With the right approach and mindset, you can achieve financial freedom and secure your financial future through stock market investing.

ISREAL JOSHUA CHUKWUBUEZE

CHAPTER THIRTEEN:

"Entrepreneurship: Building Wealth Through Starting A Business"

Entrepreneurship is a powerful tool for building wealth, but it also comes with its own set of risks and challenges. In this chapter, we'll discuss strategies for building wealth through starting a business, including how to find a profitable business idea, how to create a business plan, and how to manage risk.

1. Find a profitable business idea: The key to success in entrepreneurship is finding a profitable business idea. Research different industries and markets, and look for untapped opportunities or gaps in the market.

2. Create a business plan: Once you've identified a business idea, it's important to create a detailed business plan. This will help you define your target market, set financial goals, and map out a strategy for achieving them.

3. Secure funding: Starting a business requires capital, so it's important to secure funding from investors, banks, or other sources.

4. Build a strong team: Starting a business is challenging, and it's important to have a strong team of advisors,

mentors, and employees to support you along the way.

5. Manage risk: Starting a business is risky, and it's important to have a plan in place to manage risk. This may include diversifying your revenue streams, having a solid financial plan, and having a contingency plan in case of unexpected setbacks.

6. Stay informed: Keep up with industry trends and changes, and stay informed about any new laws, regulations, or technologies that may affect your business.

7. Be adaptable: The business environment is constantly changing, so it's important to be adaptable and willing to pivot or change course as needed.

8. Continuously educate yourself: The business world is constantly evolving, so it's important to continuously educate yourself and stay informed on new strategies and tactics.

9. Network with other entrepreneurs: Building a network of other entrepreneurs can be incredibly valuable. They can provide valuable insights, advice and even connect you to deals and opportunities that you may not have otherwise come across.

10. Have patience: Building a successful business takes time and patience. Don't get discouraged if you don't see immediate returns, and stay focused on your long-

term goals.

In conclusion, entrepreneurship is a powerful tool for building wealth, but it also comes with its own set of risks and challenges. By finding a profitable business idea, creating a detailed business plan, securing funding, building a strong team, managing risk, staying informed, being adaptable, continuously educating yourself, networking with other entrepreneurs and having patience, you can increase your chances of success as an entrepreneur. Remember to always be open to new ideas, be willing to take risks and never stop learning and growing. Building a business takes time and effort, but with the right mindset and approach, the rewards can be significant. So if you're ready to take the leap and start your own business, go for it and build the wealth you desire.

ISREAL JOSHUA CHUKWUBUEZE

CHAPTER FOURTEEN:

"Conclusion: Putting It All Together"

Congratulations on making it through our 7 easy ways to acquire great wealth. By now, you should have a solid understanding of the principles and strategies for building wealth, including saving 10% of your income, setting a budget, investing, managing risk, home ownership, retirement planning and insurance, and lifelong learning.

But, how do you put it all together and create a cohesive plan for achieving financial freedom? In this chapter, we'll discuss how to create a plan of action and make it work for you.

1. Assess your current financial situation: Before you can create a plan of action, it's important to assess your current financial situation. This includes understanding your income, expenses, assets, and debts.

2. Set financial goals: Once you understand your current financial situation, you can set specific financial goals. These should be specific, measurable, attainable, relevant, and time-bound (SMART).

3. Prioritize your goals: With your goals in mind, prioritize them based on their importance to you. This will help you focus on the most important goals first and make sure you're not spreading yourself too thin.

4. Create a budget: With your goals in mind, create a budget that will help you achieve them. Your budget should be realistic and take into account your income, expenses, and savings.

5. Invest: Investing is a powerful tool for building wealth, and it's important to include it in your plan of action. Be sure to research different investment options and create a diversified portfolio that aligns with your goals and risk tolerance.

6. Manage risk: Be sure to include risk management in your plan of action. This includes having a plan in place to protect your investments and assets.

7. Continuously educate yourself: The world of personal finance is constantly changing, so it's important to continue to educate yourself and stay informed. This includes reading books, attending seminars, or hiring a financial advisor.

8. Review and adjust: Review your progress regularly, and make adjustments as needed. Your goals and circumstances may change, so it's important to be flexible and adapt your plan accordingly.

9. Don't give up: Building wealth takes time and effort, and it's easy to get discouraged. Keep in mind that setbacks and failures are a natural part of the process, and don't give up on your goals.

10. Be consistent: Consistency is key when it comes to building wealth. Stick to your plan, be disciplined, and make sure you're taking the necessary steps to achieve your goals every day.

In conclusion, creating a plan of action and putting it all together is essential for achieving financial freedom.

By assessing your current financial situation, setting specific goals, creating a budget, investing, managing risk, continuously educating yourself, and reviewing and adjusting your plan as needed, you can work towards achieving the wealth and financial security you desire.

Remember to be consistent and don't give up, as building wealth takes time and effort. With the strategies and principles outlined in this book, you now have the tools to start on the path to financial success.

WORKBOOK SHEET OUTLINES

CHAPTER ONE: THE LAW OF 10%; SAVE 10% OF ALL INCOME

- A table that includes columns for "Income Sources", "Monthly Income", "10% Savings Goal", and "Total Savings in X years"
- A section for calculating savings goals based on different income levels
- A section for setting up a separate savings account and naming it the "Freedom Account"

CHAPTER TWO: SETTING A BUDGET: THE KEY TO CONSISTENTLY SAVING 10%

- A table that includes columns for "Income", "Expenses", "Savings", and "Remaining Income"
- A section for listing and calculating fixed expenses (rent, utilities, etc.)
- A section for listing and calculating variable expenses (shopping, entertainment, etc.)
- A section for creating a budget plan for the month

CHAPTER THREE: INVESTMENT 101: PUTTING YOUR MONEY TO WORK

- A table that includes columns for "Investment Options", "Risk Level", "Potential Return", and "Ideal Investment Timeframe"
- A section for researching and comparing different investment options
- A section for determining personal risk tolerance and investment time frame

CHAPTER FOUR: MANAGING RISK: PROTECTING YOUR INVESTMENT

- A table that includes columns for "Investment Options", "Diversification Strategies", "Risk Management Techniques"
- A section for researching and comparing different strategies for diversifying investments
- A section for implementing risk management techniques

CHAPTER FIVE: THE POWER OF HOME OWNERSHIP: BUILDING WEALTH THROUGH REAL ESTATE

- A table that includes columns for "Property Type", "Location", "Price", and "Potential Return on Investment"
- A section for researching and comparing different types of properties and locations
- A section for calculating potential return on investment

ISREAL JOSHUA CHUKWUBUEZE

CHAPTER SIX: RETIREMENT PLANNING AND INSURANCE: PROTECTING YOUR FUTURE

- A table that includes columns for "Retirement Savings Options", "Monthly Contribution", "Projected Savings at Retirement", and "Insurance Needs"
- A section for researching and comparing different retirement savings options
- A section for calculating projected retirement savings and identifying insurance needs

CHAPTER SEVEN: LIFELONG LEARNING: INCREASING YOUR EARNING POTENTIAL

- A table that includes columns for "Education and Career Goals", "Courses and Training Programs", "Costs", and "Potential Earnings Increase"
- A section for researching and comparing different education and career goals
- A section for identifying courses and training programs that align with the goals
- A section for calculating the potential earnings increase

CHAPTER EIGHT: MAXIMIZING YOUR INCOME: NEGOTIATING SALARIES AND RAISES

- A table that includes columns for "Current Salary", "Market Research", "Negotiation Techniques", "Potential Salary Increase"
- A section for researching the market and industry standards for salaries
- A section for identifying and practicing negotiation techniques
- A section for calculating potential salary increase

CHAPTER NINE: DEBT MANAGEMENT: GETTING OUT OF DEBT AND STAYING OUT

- A table that includes columns for "Type of Debt", "Interest Rate", "Minimum Monthly Payment", and "Repayment Plan"
- A section for identifying and listing all types of debt
- A section for researching and comparing different debt repayment options and creating a plan
- A section for creating a budget for paying off debt
- A section for identifying and avoiding situations that lead to accumulating more debt

CHAPTER TEN: TAX PLANNING: MAXIMIZING YOUR DEDUCTIONS AND CREDITS

- A table that includes columns for "Income", "Deductions", "Credits", "Tax Liability"
- A section for researching and identifying potential deductions and credits
- A section for calculating potential tax savings
- A section for creating a plan for maximizing deductions and credits in the future

CHAPTER ELEVEN: REAL ESTATE INVESTING: BUILDING WEALTH THROUGH PROPERTY

- A table that includes columns for "Property Type", "Location", "Price", "Potential Return on Investment", "Risks"
- A section for researching and comparing different types of properties, locations, and potential returns on investment
- A section for identifying and assessing risks

CHAPTER TWELVE: STOCK MARKET INVESTING: BUILDING WEALTH THROUGH EQUITIES

- A table that includes columns for "Stock Options", "Risk Level", "Potential Return", "Ideal Investment Timeframe"
- A section for researching and comparing different stock options
- A section for determining personal risk tolerance and investment time frame
- A section for creating a diversification strategy

CHAPTER THIRTEEN: ENTREPRENEURSHIP: BUILDING WEALTH THROUGH STARTING A BUSINESS

- A table that includes columns for "Business Idea", "Market Research", "Start-up Costs", "Potential Return on Investment"
- A section for researching and comparing different business ideas
- A section for conducting market research
- A section for calculating start-up costs and potential return on investment

CHAPTER FOURTEEN: CONCLUSION: PUTTING IT ALL TOGETHER

- A section for summarizing key takeaways from each chapter
- A section for creating a personalized wealth-building plan
- A section for setting future financial goals and tracking progress towards achieving them

www.ingramcontent.com/pod-product-compliance
Lightning Source LLC
Chambersburg PA
CBHW070305220526
45465CB00004B/1758